Black in White

Foreign body

and other poems from the
Black in White Poetry Competition 2021

CHARLOTTE SHYLLON

+ 32 contributing poets

© Charlotte Shyllon

First edition, November 2021

Second edition, August 2023

Edited by Winston Forde
Cover design by Christine Welby
Front cover illustration by Tia Diana Draws IG:@tiadianadraws

Foreign Body is the title of the winning poem in the Black in White Poetry Competition 2021, written by first prize winner Serena Malcom.

To The Good Apples. © *Jermaine Carew. Reproduced with permission from Poems from our Young, by Jermaine Carew, Esmeralda Simpson, Keira Forde, Miriam Mansaray. Edited by Winston Forde. Compiled by the WLTF Literary Agency. Published by New Generation Publishing in 2020.*

www.blackinwhiteservices.co.uk

Transforming Words Ltd. trading as *Black in White*

ISBN 978-1-78792-023-1

Book design, layout and production management by Into Print
www.intoprint.net
+44 (0)1604 832149

Second Edition

This book, originally titled Black in White Community Collection Volume 1, has been retitled Foreign Body. We have made this change for two key reasons:

- To acknowledge the first prize winner Serena Malcolm's poem from the Black in White Poetry Competition 2021.

- To ensure all of the books in the Black in White series have a clearly different identity, while remaining under the same umbrella brand.

We have also taken the opportunity to commission an illustration for the front cover from illustrator Tia Miles, of Tia Diana Draws, to reflect the title and contents of Serena's poem.

We hope you like this book's new identity and enjoy reading this powerful collection of poems by 33 poets!

CONTENTS

Section 5:
Poetry Competition: Highly Commended 81

Section 6:
About Black in White. .. .. .133

Dedication

This book is dedicated to all those who see and value the benefits of equality, diversity and inclusion, and who labour actively in whatever capacity within this field to help open the minds of those who are the reason why these poems have been written…

Acknowledgements

I would like to acknowledge several people who have been instrumental in helping me to compile the material for this book.

☺ My children, Andrew, and Olivia Coker, who have had to share their mother with her laptop all those nights and weekends when I have been working on Black in White activities.

☺ The members of the Black in White team – my sisters Hanna and Deborah, and friends Sarah Murray, Denyse Barwick, Tia Miles, and David Balfour – who have sacrificed many hours of their free time to work alongside me on this project.

☺ My fellow judges in the first Black in White Poetry Competition – Greg Evaristo, Femi Williams, and Tia Miles – who diligently undertook an iterative judging process to select the winning and highly commended poems.

☺ The guest poets and all the poetry competition entrants, especially those featured in this book. Without their poems, this book wouldn't be as content rich as it is. Sadly, not everyone could be selected and celebrated publicly, but I appreciate all their efforts.

☺ Winston Forde, whose editorial effort and support has been invaluable; Christine Welby, who designed many of the supporting materials used to promote the poetry competition and this book; Hanna and Denyse, my team at Transforming Words; and all my other family and friends, too many to mention, who gave an encouraging word or two along the way or inspired some of my poems.

☺ Most of all, I acknowledge and thank God. Like the Psalmist says, we are fearfully and wonderfully made. Even for those of a different faith (or no faith), the message to take from this is that all human life is to be esteemed and valued equally for all our similarities and differences.

FOREWORD

Dear Reader

I was both surprised and delighted to have been asked to write the Foreword to this amazing collection of poetry. Surprised because I have never actually met Charlotte; and delighted because I feel that I have come to know her through her first book of poetry, *Black in White*.

Charlotte's first collection illustrates so well what a remarkable woman she is. Through her personal and powerful poetry, Charlotte shared her lived experience of 'how it is' to become a successful Black woman working in a White corporate world. Her poems are full of insight, reflecting both the joy of success and the pain of unconscious bias and overt racism with little to no bitterness yet with a strong and powerful message of hope for change.

Charlotte's second book of poetry, *Black in White Community Collection*, is a compilation of hers and others poetry. Charlotte's voice and the voices of others can be heard loud and clear through the lived, and often painful, experience of each of the expressive contributors. What is clear is that we still have much to do as a society to address the disparities and inequalities that exist.

Sadly, inequalities and racism are still an everyday facet of our society and few, if any, institutions are immune from them. Nevertheless, there are signs that things are moving in a positive direction. A growing number of organisations have openly committed to systematically investigate inequality in all its forms to acknowledge, understand and tackle structural inequalities that affect both individuals and groups working within and for them. Recognising how we got here and what needs to be done to ensure equity, inclusion and belonging for all, particularly for those who are marginalised, underrepresented and excluded is key.

Black in White and *Black in White Community Collection* are a must read for anyone who wishes to understand the impact of racism, intentional or otherwise, through the words of those who experience it. Through the powerful poetry in this new book, you will vicariously experience what it means to be Black in a predominantly White world.

I would like to take this opportunity to publically say a huge thank you to Charlotte and all the contributors to this glorious book of poetry. Thank you for inspiring, provoking and stimulating the very necessary conversations to help us on our journey to effect change. By opening our hearts and minds to the experiences of others we may be able to move beyond the rhetoric to making the world a better and more just place.

I hope that when you read Charlotte's books you too will be inspired to be part of that change!

Anna Kyprianou, Chartered CCIPD CMgr CCMI
Pro Vice-Chancellor for Equality, Diversity and Inclusion
Middlesex University

INTRODUCTION

What inspired *'Black in White Community Collection'*?

The power of motivation

I always knew I had a book or two inside me. In fact, like many of us, I'd had an urge to write a book for decades. I'd even started writing one or two, only for them to lie unfinished and half-forgotten in a 'hobbies' folder.

I never imagined my first book would be a poetry book, even though I'd always enjoyed poetry at school. I remember some of the poems I learned back then that made an impact on me; Wordsworth's *'I wandered lonely as a cloud that floats on high o'er vales and hills…'* is still a firm favourite.

The first book I started seriously to write was about business etiquette. I believe that these days some people eschew several basic rules in the workplace because they've never been taught them. The second book I started to write is about my family history, to help our future generations know about their forebears. Even in these days when genealogy and family history records can reveal much about our ancestry, our oral histories often become inaccessible as each generation expires.

I'm still hopeful that both of those books will see the light of day, one of these days.

The context above is useful because it demonstrates what a powerful force motivation is. Although I clearly lacked the motivation to push through with my earlier book attempts, when I wrote my first book *Black in White* last year, it took me less than two months to produce the contents and another three months or so to publish it. Why was I so motivated on this occasion to start and complete my book? One now very inspirational name: George Floyd.

As my nephew who was eight years old at the time said during my virtual book launch event in May, *"If you don't know who George Floyd is, you must have been living under a rock!"*. His name and sad demise are known by millions of us across the globe following his murder by a policeman in Minneapolis, Minnesota who put his knee on George's throat for 9 minutes and 29 seconds. A life tragically and wastefully expunged because of a store clerk's *suspicion* that George had used a counterfeit $20 note.

The time the police came for me

My horror and outrage at that unjust act was heightened by the fact that it could have been me. Seriously. Albeit in a different time and space, I too have had the police descend on me in a public place because of a suspicion that I had committed a crime. Thankfully, it happened just once, a long time ago, but this is the first time I have related the story outside of my immediate circle of family and friends.

Some 20 years ago, my sister Deborah and I met up to have a manicure and afterwards went to a fast-food restaurant in Victoria for a bite to eat. We stood in line, as we Brits do, waiting to be served. It was a Saturday afternoon, and the place was heaving with long queues and lots of people in a confined space.

At some point, a group of young boys came in and were being a bit boisterous. They bumped into a few people but smiled and said sorry, so no one seemed to mind too much. But my sister and I rolled our eyes and clutched our handbags a bit tighter.

We ordered our food and went to the basement level of the restaurant to consume our burgers, chips and milkshakes and chat about our lives. Compared to the upper level, it was relatively quiet with only a few other people down there. A little while later, a man wearing a white shirt, heavy duty shoes and carrying nothing more than a solitary drink came down the stairs and sat nearby, all alone. Something just didn't seem quite right about him, so I whispered jokingly to my sister that he might be an undercover cop.

Little did I know how right I was! Disrobed of his jacket, helmet and epaulettes, he was a PC who'd been sent down as an advance party, we subsequently discovered, to keep an eye on us. Suddenly the basement filled with several police officers – about eight of them. A couple came up to my sister and me. They told us another customer had reported that his wallet had been stolen while he had been queuing to buy some food; because we'd been standing close to him, he'd claimed it must have been us!

Playing the 'privilege card'

Honestly, my first reaction was to laugh at this absurd allegation – but it was no laughing matter. Absolutely horrified, I wasted no time in telling the police they had made a big mistake. In the most cultured tones I could muster, I explained that not only was I a well-paid public relations executive, but I was also the daughter of a former diplomat and had been educated at one of the UK's top public schools. Now of course no one is above committing a crime, irrespective of their upbringing – but I hoped that by ensuring they knew my sister and I were black people from a privileged background, it might give them pause for thought. How sad that I felt I had to play the 'privilege card' – but frankly it was just the judicious use of a card I had been dealt in life.

At that point they apologised, and I overheard one of them mutter to another, 'I think we're barking up the wrong tree here'. But my sister and I still had to suffer the indignity of being taken to the restaurant toilets where we had to remove our coats so they could search us and check our handbags. We were innocent, so naturally they didn't find any stolen property on us. We told them that the most likely culprits were the groups of boys who'd come into the restaurant acting suspiciously – which they could see for themselves if they looked at the CCTV footage. Oh, and by the way, those boys were white… funny how they hadn't registered as potential culprits to our accuser, but my sister and I – two adult black women with manicured nails – had.

Even though we weren't arrested, the restaurant staff treated us appallingly when we went back upstairs, blocked us from the till area and rudely told us to get out; we were leaving anyway! When I wrote to their CEO to complain, I received a bunch of flowers and vouchers for their restaurants. I never redeemed those vouchers; though a nice gesture, they were hardly compensation for what my sister and I had been through! That incident scarred me, and I didn't go back into that fast food chain again for many years, when the pain and shame of that nightmare experience had somewhat diminished.

Airing other people's stories

The thing is, perversely, I now think how lucky I'd been! Unlike George Floyd and the thousands of other innocent black people who have been victims of police brutality, I escaped with nothing more than my wounded pride.

Despite this book being ostensibly about racism at work (we're getting to that soon, I promise), much of this introduction so far has been about racism in our everyday lives, and specifically at the hands of the police. I make no apologies for this because, as I said earlier, George Floyd's story was a powerful motivation for me and many others to speak up about our experiences of racism.

As black people living in a predominantly white society, most of us can tell a tale or two about how racism impinges on our daily existence. That's why in addition to telling my own stories, I am also keen to air other people's stories in their own voices. This was the driving force behind the launch of the Black in White Poetry Competition. It's also why, in this book, as well as all the winning and highly commended poems from our first poetry competition – which are for the most part work-related, by the way – I have included five poems from guest poets telling their stories too.

Tragically for Alim Kamara, one of the guest poets whose song lyrics *Tell Me* are included in this book, his cousin Sheku lost his life while in police custody. When I watched Alim's heart-rending performance of this song online I was moved to tears and anger in equal measures. Yet in any profession, there are lots of good eggs among the rotten ones – and the same is true in the police force. Another of our guest poets Jermaine Carew's poem *To The Good Apples* is a powerful call for action by the good to influence the evil.

Guest poet Tia Miles describes how she feels as a mixed-race person living in Britain in her epic eponymous poem. Meanwhile in guest poet Tré Ventour's poem *White Persuasions*, he paints a very vivid picture of why as a young black boy growing up and seeing white skin as the epitome of normalcy, he'd wanted so much to be white.

My final guest poet is William Johnson, whom I commissioned specifically to write a poem about racism at work. What he has delivered is a potent exposé of some of his experiences and a rallying call for change.

Why workplace perspectives?

The subject of William's poem allows me to shift gears into why we need to tackle workplace racism. My first book, *Black in White*, contains poems describing some of my experiences of racism, prejudice, unconscious bias and microaggressions in the workplace. I also wrote a few poems about other people's experiences. I chose to focus on racism in the workplace because I feel that this is an area where these incidents happen, yet often don't get dealt with or even spoken about.

In the immediate aftermath of George Floyd's murder, the world was moved, even shamed to voice support for stamping out racism and, in some cases, to take positive action on equality, diversity and inclusion (EDI). There has been some progress towards change, in pockets, over the last 18 months – but it's clear that many people have also simply settled back into life as it was before since the world's focus has shifted to other things.

That's why we need to continue to make noise about racism in the workplace. As part of the marketing effort around the *Black in White Poetry Competition*, I wrote the short poem below (slightly tweaked since) and produced a video with the other judges, saying two lines each:

It's time to write your poetic story,
Of racism at work, whether subtle or gory.
We must keep teaching that racism is wrong,
We must continue to bang the gong.
Send your poems to Black in White,
And we can help to shed some light.
You may get a prize and, what's more
Prove racism is real, not folklore.

This book – a collection of poems I have written together with 32 other poets who either submitted entries into the poetry competition or provided one on request as guest poets – is designed to help educate and encourage action against racism. Action is needed, and sustained action at that. Since publishing my first book, I have provided EDI counsel to several companies, been co-chair of a new diversity and inclusion award category, written articles and given presentations on the topic. There is still a lot to do, and I intend to continue to do whatever I can do.

People of all races, colours and creed need to take an anti-racist stance, and challenge and call out racism in the workplace, and beyond, whenever and wherever it occurs. Change will only come if we all see it as our individual responsibility. As Barak Obama said: *'Change will not come if we wait for some other person or some other time. We are the ones we've been waiting for. We are the change that we seek.'*

SECTION 1:

About the Black in White Poetry Competition 2021

Black in White
Poetry
Competition 2021

After the release of *Black in White* in November 2020 and its official launch in May 2021, I decided to run a poetry competition knowing that there is still a lot of work to be done to open eyes to, and change minds about, the spectre of racism. Having already told some of my stories of racism in the workplace in *Black in White*, giving other people an opportunity to air some of their experiences of racism in their own voices was an obvious next step.

I am blessed to have around me a team of staff and volunteers who supported the launch of *Black in White*, and who were eager to continue with me on this journey. You can 'meet' this amazing group of people in Section 6 of this book. They played a key role in helping establish *Black in White* as a viable company and in getting things up and running, including attending Zoom calls every Saturday morning and many Wednesday evenings.

The first Black in White Poetry Competition was open for entries from late June to mid-August 2021. Although lots of poetry competitions are run successfully by a single judge, I felt it would be important to bring in other minds with a range of different perspectives to help identify the best entries, since everyone's response to poetry is so personal. I was fortunate to secure three brilliant individuals, Greg Evaristo, Femi Williams and Tia Miles, to join me on the judging panel (see their biographies below).

The judges reviewed all the poems anonymously. Judging involved a detailed initial sift of all the poems we received followed by individual first round scoring by each of the judges of the 70+ shortlisted poems against six criteria: beauty, power, education or entertainment; technical excellence;

form and flow; choice of words and readability; overall impact; and polish and expertise (adapted from *https://allpoetry.com/column/7522123-How-To-Rate-and-Judge-Poetry--by-Grandpa-Moses*). The individual scores were then summarised, and poems were listed in order based on the total scores they received. During a judging day Zoom call in mid-September, we selected our three winners and 25 highly commended entries.

We announced the results on 15th September on the Black in White website and social media channels – a pretty impressive three-month turn-around. It then took a further two months to produce this book and launch it to the world. What a worthwhile and whirlwind experience it has been!

From the off, I have said this is the first Black in White Poetry Competition. Check. We will be running a bigger and better competition in 2022, so watch this space.

My co-judges' biographies are below:

❖ **Greg Evaristo** is a non-executive board director for Bonnier Books UK, contributing to its people strategy, with a particular focus on the ongoing development of its diversity and inclusion plan. He has 30 years' experience in senior roles within the book publishing industry and founded the leading book publishing executive search agency, Gregory Martin Search. Before that he ran an executive coaching and talent development business that coached senior level book publishing executives. His sister is Bernardine Evaristo the prizewinning author.

❖ **Femi Williams** (aka Femi Fem) kicked off his career running the Family Funktion/Shake & Fingerpop warehouse parties, with Norman Jay & Judge Jules. In 1990, he set up the ground-breaking Young Disciples with Marco Nelson featuring Carleen Anderson. Responding to the demand, Femi began writing, producing and remixing for a wide range of artists. Alongside this work, his public profile as a headline DJ and promoter made his face well-known. Discography: Eye of the Sun, Elevate, Solace.

❖ **Tia Miles** is a poet, singer/song writer and spoken word artist from East London. After George Floyd's death in 2020, she wrote and performed a poem called *My name is Tia*, which received over 6,000 views on social media. Tia has performed spoken word poetry at various venues across London. Tia has featured in some of FELA. Mi's songs and music videos, and designs his album covers. By day, Tia works in the finance industry and owns a digital illustration business.

Greg Evaristo provides some comments on the Black in White Poetry Competition from his perspective as a judge:

Poetry is such a powerful art form as it enables the writer to freely express themselves using creative language to evoke in the reader an emotional pull or to fire up an imagination with what they have to say.

The best poetry is always nuanced and can move the reader and like layers of an onion you get a greater sense of its meaning the deeper you delve into the poem with each reading.

I believe that the inaugural Black in White Poetry Competition is a very welcome and refreshing addition to the poetry calendar as it gives the perfect platform to new voices from underrepresented people of colour to express their unique experiences in the British workplace and beyond.

Judging this year's competition – along with my fellow judges – was both enjoyable and enlightening. The overall standard of entries was very good especially as most were not poets but ordinary folks. All felt they had something to say on how the lack of inclusiveness and representation affected them at work and chose the form of a poem to express this.

What came across clearly within each entry was the passion, sometimes visceral emotion, the often silent suffering and pain they felt at the treatment they endured whilst in the world of work. The winning poem and runners up were all worthy winners.

Toni Morrison was once asked what's the definition of a poet is; she replied *"it's someone who writes poetry"*, so I hope that our winners will continue to write poetry by expressing themselves with this wonderful art form.

SECTION 2:

Charlotte's Poems

It is an irrefutable fact that I have experienced workplace racism and unconscious bias. In some of the situations there was no tangible evidence, just a 'knowing' that my skin colour played a part in something that went down. The people involved would probably have denied it and might even have been outraged that anyone could suggest they were motivated by anything other than professionalism. Therein lies the challenge – to say something and risk that kind of pious denial of responsibility or worse, say nothing to avoid any negative outcome thereby allowing these sorts of issues to continue. We have to stop being intimidated by the 'what ifs' and speak out against the scourge of racism.

The six poems in this section are all true stories, written by me. One is an account of a personal experience, and one is derived from a situation that I faced. The other four are based on incidents related to me by dependable friends. Most are in the narrative-style of rhyming poems because that's what I enjoy writing the most. I hope they resonate and provide helpful insights.

SHE CRIED AND I WAS FINISHED

She wanted me to cave in
When we split our business win.
She insisted on the lion's share.
When I said no, she didn't care.

So, because she didn't get her way,
She fought dirty to win the day.
To hoodwink our boss, she made a plan
To paint me as an angry black man.

Her scheme wasn't obvious.
Or maybe I was just oblivious
To the tactic she chose to deploy
Just because I'd stood firm and wasn't coy.

Perhaps I should have guessed
That my reputation had been messed.
But when someone said he'd seen her crying,
How could I know my bacon was frying?

She was the darling of the business.
A group head like me but, nevertheless,
Her impact was out of my ballpark,
Though I tried my best to make a mark.

After our chat, I thought things had died down,
But whenever I saw her, she would just frown.
Then it became clear at a meeting with my boss
How she had ensured I'd be at a loss!

My boss told me that I should say sorry
For making her cry, for not sharing the glory.
But when I disagreed and wasn't contrite,
That's when things got really tight!

Several weeks later, HR got involved,
From then on, things quickly evolved.
Before long I was thrown out on my ear,
Tossed on the scrap heap without a care.

Finally, I understood what she had done.
Too late, by then, because I was gone!
But though she meant to do me wrong,
Guess what? It only made me strong!

Quotable Quotes

Diversity is being invited to the party; inclusion is being asked to dance.

Verna Myers

Inclusion and fairness in the workplace... is not simply the right thing to do; it's the smart thing to do.

Alexis Herman

What's often ignored is that diversity is not only a pipeline or recruiting issue. It's an issue of making the people who do make it through the pipeline want to stay at your company.

Andrea Barrica

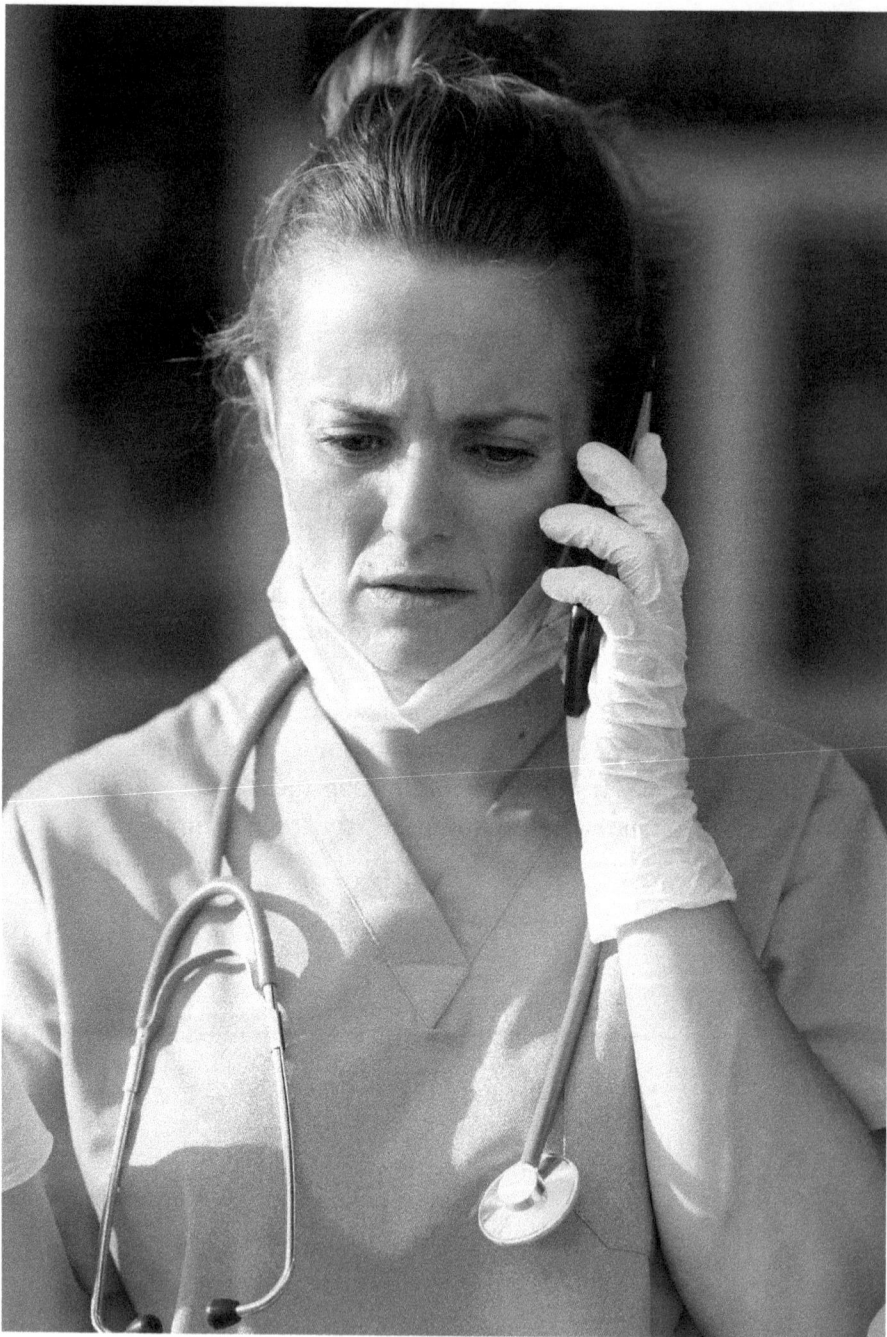

A TASTE OF RACISM

I'm British and I'm white
so, you'd be within your right
to ask me how I could truly know,
how racism makes you feel so low?

I know as an ally, I can sympathise.
But I've tasted racism so can empathise
because one day someone shouted at me:
'Hey, go back to your own country!'

She actually said it over the phone,
so couldn't see I was cut to the bone,
or that, being British and white,
I was left reeling by her spite.

She was a patient in the NHS
in a part of Birmingham, I must confess,
where many people of colour reside;
white, brown, black, living side by side.

Many help keep vital health services going,
so, she'd just assumed, without even knowing,
that my local accent was simply masking
a different skin colour – and she wasn't asking!

If she'd seen me, my white privilege
would've protected me from such sacrilege.
That privilege is unmerited, it's not how it should be;
you only enjoy it if you look like me.

But in that moment, I felt it dearly:
the ugly face of racism, exposed clearly.
I slammed the phone down with haste.
I know I'd only had a little taste.

Such racism is daily staple food for you
if your skin is black – it must make you feel blue.
That's why we all need to be educated,
the benefits of learning not under-rated.

Equity and justice must be our goal,
diversity and inclusion in every role.
In work, in life, in everything,
kick racism out, respect is king.

Quotable Quotes

Many conversations about diversity and inclusion do not happen in the boardroom because people are embarrassed at using unfamiliar words or afraid of saying the wrong thing — yet this is the very place we need to be talking about it. The business case speaks for itself — diverse teams are more innovative and successful in going after new markets

Inga Beale

Strength lies in differences, not in similarities

Stephen Covey

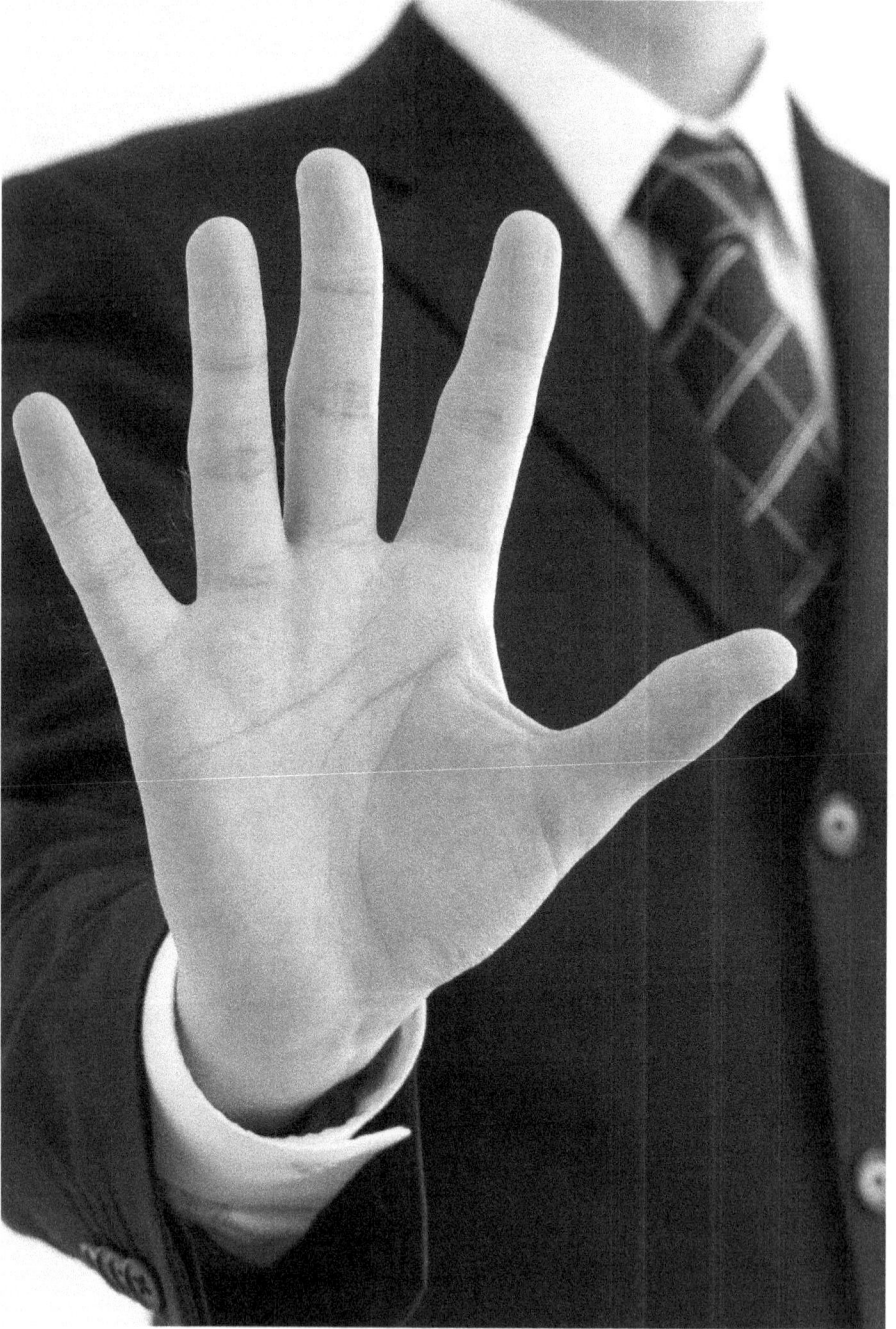

LET'S KEEP IN TOUCH

You'd been my boss for three years, an older gent,
When you suddenly announced your retirement.
I went along with the shock all expressed,
But to be really honest, I just felt blessed.

We're good at pretending we're just like you.
It's what some of us black people do.
For that, some might call me a coconut,
But it helps me to keep the 'race' door shut.

To me, it's a matter of playing the game,
Of appearing to be just the same.
I'd become quite adept at it –
I'd turn on the charm, you'd smile at my wit.

When working, you'd often seek my advice.
You took it and used it more than once or twice.
But every so often you'd put me in my place,
Show me who's boss – a real slap in the face!

Your controlling ways left me feeling blue,
But what was I supposed to do?
I needed to work to pay my bills
So couldn't engage in a battle of wills.

Then when you said that you were leaving,
Though a big sigh of relief I was heaving
I decided to say something nice, in fact
Words I now wish I could retract.

'Let's keep in touch,' I said sincerely
And was truly shocked when you said clearly
That keeping in touch wasn't to be
Because you no longer needed me.

Since I now know you were a fake,
Did you really love my sister's rum cake?
When you professed to love R&B music
Was it something in fact you couldn't stick?

Perhaps you were code-switching, in a different code.
Perhaps you'd seen me as a bump in your road.
But with your true colours fully on show,
My true colours you'll never know.

Quotable Quotes

I have a dream that my four little children will one day live in a nation where they will not be judged by the colour of their skin but by the content of their character.

Martin Luther King, Jr.

Diversity: the art of thinking independently together.

Malcolm Forbes

THE REAL PHARMACIST

I was 22, black, female, employed,
As a pharmacy locum I'd been deployed.
Busy at work in a dispensary one morning,
An incident occurred with no forewarning.

A woman came in needing advice.
Ordinary looking, she seemed quite nice.
She had a query giving her some bother.
It wasn't for her, but for her mother.

The assistant asked me to speak with her.
I said, 'No problem, I'll be right there.'
When I approached her, it was with a smile
Because I knew she's been waiting a while.

On her face all I saw was confusion,
Just like someone who'd had a contusion.
'How can I help you?' was what I said
She looked askance and shook her head:

'I want to speak to the pharmacist,
The real pharmacist – I must insist.'
'I'm the real pharmacist,' I replied politely.
Her shock was clear, as she shuddered slightly.

When I pointed to my certificate on the wall,
She looked at me like she'd tasted gall!
Pulling herself together, but still looking stressed,
She said: 'Your parents must be so impressed!'

Oblivious to why she'd said this to me
I blithely replied: 'Not my family!
They'd wanted me to achieve a lot more.
If I'd been a doctor, I'd have been top drawer!'

The lesson to take from this old tale
Is that being black, young and female
Means sometimes you're not recognised,
In a society somewhat homogenised.

But let no one's opinion define who you are.
If you want it, you can be a star!
You can rise to the top in your profession.
Sister, let that be your confession!

Quotable Quotes

It is time for parents to teach young people early on that in diversity there is beauty and there is strength.

Maya Angelou

There's a pure and simple business case for diversity:
Companies that are more diverse are more successful.

Mindy Grossman

HOW MANY TIMES MUST I PROVE MYSELF?

I have the career experience and track-record
For most people to recognise I have many first-rate skills.
I have some of the best brands in the industry on my CV,
Global, high-profile companies where I've worked and succeeded.

My success should make me eligible for being a CEO.
Yet despite input from industry leaders who mentor me,
Somehow it has eluded me, time and time again.
How many times must I prove myself to you?

Do you scrutinise and question everyone equally?
Do you make all candidates jump through the same hoops?
Even for a position for which I am over-qualified,
Why am I often good enough till it comes down to the last two?

Your diversity and inclusion policies read impressively;
Words carefully crafted to allay concerns and appear progressive.
But the blockades are there, invisible, intangible,
Making failure to attain that top spot my reality.

My reality that as a black woman with a 1st class honours degree,
With an MBA and an Oxbridge postgrad qualification,
I must settle and get comfortable under that glass ceiling.
Or not. I've never been comfortable with allowing anyone to limit me.

But moving out and trying to make it on my own is no panacea.
Being a self-appointed black female CEO comes with its own challenges;
Because to win the most lucrative contracts and secure the best deals,
I must continue to prove myself, time and time again…

YOU PICKED ON THE WRONG GUY

Every weekday morning, come rain or shine,
waiting for the train in this Surrey town of mine,
I'm smartly dressed, one of many commuters
travelling into the city with our computers.

I kept my head down, like everyone else there,
I was on my phone, in my own sphere.
You came onto the platform and looked around,
our eyes met briefly, you smiled, I frowned.

From your unkempt look, I knew you wanted money.
Sure enough, you came over like a bee to honey.
I'm generous, but won't support anyone's habit,
It's one time you can call me crabbit*.

I said no, politely – then firmly but you didn't go.
I can't be the only one to have ever said so,
but you clearly didn't like to hear it from me.
As you spewed racist abuse, I felt all at sea.

Not a single commuter came to help me,
or told you to back off and leave me be.
Emboldened, your abuse continued unabated,
your eyes hate-filled, your voice aggravated.

The next day, you continued to be a pain,
threatened me physically on the train,
forced me to defend myself from you;
what else was I supposed to do?

I got to work and called the men in blue,
I wanted to ensure you'd get your due.
Before long we had made a plan
that they would issue you with a ban.

The next day, when you abused me again,
I sat on the train, no stress, no strain.
Two stations later, the train was invaded,
By ten police officers it was raided.

The police asked me to point you out.
I really felt like a man with clout.
As they took you off, you stopped your defiling,
as I continued my journey, I was smiling.

When swearing at me you'd felt pretty fly,
unaware you picked on the wrong guy.
You may have misjudged me because I'm black,
but I used my smarts to fight back!

---

* *Crabbit is an old Scottish slang word bad-tempered or grumpy. It's also used in Krio, a lingua franca in Sierra Leone, where it means tight-fisted.*

SECTION 3:
Guest Poems

In this section, I am delighted to include poems by five poets, three of whom have given us permission to reproduce existing content and two who wrote their poems specifically for inclusion in this book. My original intention was to only include poems about workplace racism in this book. But we have ended up with poems that tackle other relevant topics, and I believe that makes the contents of this book all the richer.

Two poems, by Alim Kamara and Jermaine Carew, are about issues many black people, especially young black men, face with the police. I don't need to go into details about institutional racism – you'd have to be viewing the world through rose-tinted specs not to be able to see how extensively it infuses most of our institutions in the UK. Suffice it to say, we still have a long way to go.

Two further poems, by Tré Ventour and Tia Miles, are about some of their experiences and feelings as young black people growing up in the UK. These demonstrate how racism continues to blight our lives and can mess with our very souls if we let it.

Finally, William Johnson's poem focuses on episodes of racism he encountered in different work settings over the years in what he aptly labels 'an arduous marathon race' and what's needed 'to keep this racial bubble shrinking'.

Read on and be inspired...

TELL ME

By Alim Kamara

Hands cuffed, feet locked
We cried when life stopped
Shut down like robots
Yeah, we know some bad cops
Did you see the full extent of injuries?
Bruv, they get to snatch a life and then keep their mouth shut.

Don't blame the rollers for taking the pain to opus
You cowards are an omen swore to protect LIARS
You killed our brother, officer
All for your co-worker

We know she had a case that needed to disappear
So she faked it to hospital
Stumbling blaming Sheku
That boy was on his last
Here's a threat, mind your step!
Coz we pray hard like we're in debt
When you're seen as prey
God and zeal are all you have left

Since you can't breathe my brother
Let me speak your breath
Until we get some justice
It will be hard to rest
Mus, I'm sorry that day I couldn't make the christening
Before the batons, Mr officer
Did he scream?

Tell me it's a dream
(I can't stand this)
Tell me it's a dream
(I shouldn't have to)
Tell me it's a dream
(I can't bear this)
Soon I wake up
(Where are you?)

The story gets even deeper
As the morning unfolds
Had to pause before I offload
Cause this twisted law of ours just left us cold
Welcome to at least what?
9 officers at the show
Within 15, it said you were out cold
Still doctors had to beg them
Remove the shackles!

I know it's graphical
But I swore at his grave
After seeing Isaac who was only 3 months throw up.
I'd fight back.
I hugged Aunty Ami and held it back
She was here to meet her grandson
Look at that

Four officers went to Colette's
Two snuck in the kitchen
The other two kept asking for dirt
For what reason?

Still they hadn't told her nothing
Took her keys, claimed
The home was now the crime scene
And all this time they hadn't told her Sheku was gone yet
And when they did,
Brace yourself!
Pepper sprays and CS as well?

Tell me it's a dream
(I can't stand this)
Tell me it's a dream
(I shouldn't have to)
Tell me it's a dream
(I can't bear this)
Soon I wake up
(Where are you?)

Now Sheku was pronounced dead around 9am
After one secret police meeting two CIDs would amend
'A member of the public found your partner bleeding
and weak, and though they called an ambulance
He died in the street'
This is real talk at 11, Colette lost it
That's when they told us Shek's best friend was a suspect

Over seven hours before we knew
Because their gaffer gave 'em permission as pressure brews
Then they had to cheek to tell the fam
Don't speak to the news.
And ran this headline,
'Six-foot black man with a knife', owh!'

He was 5'4 four with no previous and a father of two
No statements or suspensions
This could happen to you.

They even sent lawyers to bully us
But we stubborn like roots
Death in police custody
We deserve the truth
Hey you,
Tyler wants to grow up to be Spider Man so
We can climb up the heavens to get his Dad, damn!
Wake up...

Contact Alim: alimkamara.com/; IG: @alimkamara; YT: AlimKamara

Quotable Quotes

We have a very diverse environment and a very inclusive culture, and those characteristics got us through the tough times. Diversity generated a better strategy, better risk management, better debates, and better outcomes.

Alan Joyce

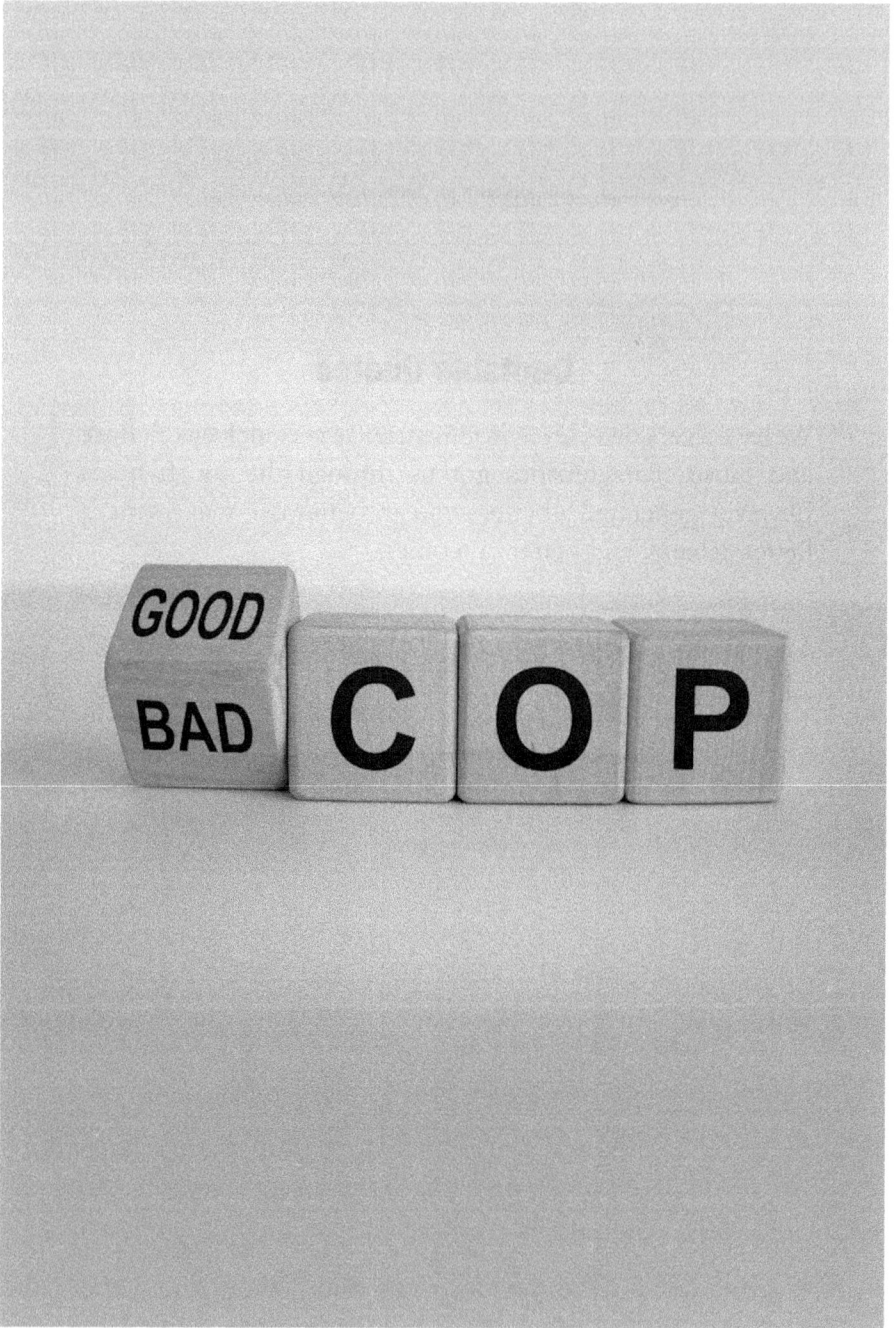

TO THE GOOD APPLES

By Jermaine Carew

This query is not for the accused,
nor the ones who beat civilians and abuse.
Those individuals need not be named,
for their actions were already videotaped and more
mention would only increase their fame.
They are the bad apples that are to blame.

This query, however, is for the rest of the barrel.
The good apples who work with the bad to help those in peril,
who demand respect when organisational problems are reported
by guys like Darrell.
Who lay down their lives every day,
who are called to serve from June to May.

I know you feel that the coverage of you is unfair,
but please bear with my civilian query if you care.
One similarity I believe that we both share,
Is that we want to be acknowledged and praised for our humanity
instead of fear.
I argue that you are most protected in society under law,
that any assault against you would be criminal
with no context line to draw.

In court, your presence is of an authority without flaw.
you are seen as the guardian of our community,
who stops folks that see chaos as an opportunity?
I argue that you knew the bad apples' ploy,
but you either stay away or watch them destroy.

You dislike generalisations yet your tactics are the same
when deployed,
your fraternal camaraderie can have a few flaws that contribute
to the endless brutal void.

Nuance is the bridge of different thoughts.
I know I have not walked in your shoes full of cuts,
I know you fear for your life constantly on duty,
But not all thugs wear a hoodie.
Your career is to protect and not to make me fear of being dead,
you are supposed to call those apples out
when they behave like Judge Dredd.

Rank and hierarchy mean nothing to a civilian life,
when a knee on the neck is enough to end constant strife.
Why is it serene without any justice?
Why does my look invite violence to you and not peace?
History marks no space for the silent gods,
ask anyone in any of the neighbourhoods.

I implore you to hold your comrades when they're irresponsible,
we all want to feel safe around the big, strong constable.
You are not the true villain, but neither the true hero,
progress does not move forward if your actions remain zero.

To the good apples that look at me, I plead that you keep trying,
do not over consume what the system is lying.
You live two lives, there is no need to choose one.
Remember which side you are on at the barrel of a gun.
Hopefully soon, if there is a hint or clue,
we would not associate beating and killing with being black and blue.

Contact Jermaine: jermainecarew@gmail.com

Quotable Quotes

We all want something to offer. This is how we belong. It's how we feel included. So if we want to include everyone, we have to help everyone develop their talents and use their gifts for the good of the community. That's what inclusion means - everyone is a contributor. And if they need help to become a contributor, then we should help them, because they are full members in a community that supports everyone.

Melinda Gates

Sports are a great place to show that equality can happen.

Venus Williams

MY NAME IS TIA

By Tia Miles

I don't want to call this my story, but I have some things to say. I'll start with who I am, a mixed-race girl from the slums. I grew up in a council flat with my sister and my mum. Who's white by the way, like the whitest woman you'll meet. Who says things like "Cor blimey, I'm hank Marvin! Should we get something to eat?"

My dad's no different when I think about it. But my dad is **black**. Born in the 60's which let's face it, is a different complication.

Because he came from a generation

of people born with aggravation

because his roots are segregation

all caused by pigmentation.

And there's me, a 50/50 mix of both.

"You sound really posh for a black girl you know". "The way you carry yourself it really doesn't show". "Which one of your parents is black? Your dad?" "Did your mum raise you alone? It can't be that bad". "Where are you from?". "I mean your parents?" "You can't be British… cause you're **BLACK**".

Where do I stand? Because I don't "sound black", I don't "act black" but I sure do look it.

So tell me – is it my curly hair, tanned skin or my "negro nose", that makes you think I should go straight back to the country in which my grandfather rose, just because I'm **black**?

That drink, you threw at me that night, out of pure spite because I'm not white. How do you think that made me feel? Do you now understand that racism is real?

Where do I stand?

Melanin – The pigment responsible for the darkness of the skin, hair, and eyes.

I have more melanin than you do, but does that make it a crime?

My name is Tia Miles.

Contact Tia: IG: @tiadiana_draws

WHITE PERSUASIONS *(After 'What Do Women Want?' by Kim Addonizio)*

By Tré Ventour

When I was kid,
I hated my skin colour
I wanted to be White
it looked like good times,
shiny and expensive. I wanted to
wrap myself in unearned advantages
like 24-carat gold. I wanted
to go to the supermarket
without moving heads,
those pound-shop soldiers
forming lies and racial stereotypes.

I wanted to be White without
the prying eyes of Kens and Margarets
in their White gaze. I wanted
to walk down British streets free from
thoughts on White terror and coloniality
to be able walk past charity shops without
thinking about White saviours and aid work
then, I wanted to wear that pale skin
like I'm on holiday in a loose flowery shirt

I wanted to be White real bad
existing with no rules. My White friends
wore society on their chest
those crest-like coats of arms
teaching White children to devour planets
when I find that White privilege,
it will be *thanks, but no thanks*
pulling Lord Blanco Epidermis
from his plinth all flimsy and cheap.

Contact Tré: treventour.com; TW: @treventoured; IG: @treventoured

RACISM IN THE WORKPLACE

By William Johnson

Racism in the work environment is rife
and can be subtle or directly to your face
Snide comments, racial stereotypes, little whispers
are all now commonplace
Many people suffer racism every day, belittled
because of their race, colour, or creed
What some racists do not understand, is that it's the same colour
we all bleed

My first real job was in McDonalds,
where I was placed in the kitchen to fry and cook
The whole of the front till was non-ethnic,
while me and my brothers never had a look
I wanted to be on the main floor with the customers,
but my boss had other ideas
He seemed to look down on me disapprovingly and
his intentions seemed more clear
He thought I was best in the kitchen without even giving me
the chance I was due
A few months passed; the new manager came in, shook things up
with his liberal view
Everybody was given the option to try different areas
and I was able to start once more
Where I excelled in my role, was given a promotion
and was mentally able to even the score

My next experience was more unconscious
where my white friend used to call everyone names
Working in the cinema, it was part and parcel where we had fun,
pranking, and playing games
I didn't think my name was special as he used to call me Fergal
as in the singer Fergal Sharkey
But it took over a year for me to consciously realise that
what he meant rhymed with Darkie
Another past friend who I worked closely with seemed
accepting of me being a black man
But looks can be deceiving and it's when I asked her on a date,
that my problems began
She told me that her family would never accept me,
which showed more cons than pros
Yet the final straw was when she said she wouldn't date black
because we all had a big nose

A few years later sitting in a café near work enjoying my lunch
of traditional pie and mash
Suddenly a customer in his thirties ran outside to his car
in a frenzied and crazy mad dash
His car was about to be ticketed by a traffic warden for illegally
parking on a double yellow line
He argued with him for a few minutes but his efforts were truly
in vain and in total decline
He came back into the café raging like a bull because he felt
that he had totally been played
He then promptly shouted and in the clearest voice
called the traffic warden "A bloody Spade"
As I was the only black man in there, people looked at me
and put their heads down in shame
As I left, the café owner came to me apologised,
even though she was not the one to blame

We now have the Black Lives Matter movement, which is slowly
picking up momentum and pace
Change won't happen overnight because we are no longer in a
sprint, but an arduous marathon race
We will need to educate more openly in order to eradicate
people's backward words and thinking
Becoming one world of harmony, love, and empathy in order to
keep this racial bubble shrinking

SECTION 4:

Poetry Competition:
Winning Poems

Our three winning poems were all unanimously and anonymously se-
lected by the judges as their favourites. Here's what judge Tia Miles had to
say about them:

It was bittersweet to read through all the experiences the talented poets
who submitted their work for Black in White's first ever poetry competition
have had of racism and discrimination both inside and outside of the
workplace. As I worked my way through the entries, I realised that racism
is not a thing of the past and if anything, it's a bigger issue than we are
aware of.

   The way I see it, poetry is art, and art is difficult to judge because it's so
subjective to the viewer. I used the list of criteria provided as part of the
judging process and judged as accurately as I could and based on that, we
have three fantastic winning poems.

   I was blown away by the winning poet, Serena Malcolm. Serena
submitted three poems, two of which left me speechless. *Foreign Body* is
powerful, informative, and creative in so many ways. The flow that this
poem is written in made it easy to read and made me feel as though I was
performing it myself! One of the highly commended poems also belongs
to Serena and is entitled *Token Black Friend*. These poems are examples
of storytelling genius, taking you on a journey from beginning to end,
using carefully placed metaphors to paint this vivid picture of Serena's
experiences of racism.

   Moving on to our second and third placed poems, we begin to see some
different perspectives and different writing styles. *Equality, Diversity, Inclusion
& Me* by Poetry Girl touches on the COMMON issues of systemic racism
in today's world. Her plainly, but powerfully-put statements, demonstrate
the harsh realities of being a black woman in a corporate world. This poem
is perfectly placed in Charlotte's *Black in White Community Collection*, as it
continues the conversation of racism in the workplace.

   Douglas Kingsley Medland, brought a wave of emotions as I read his
poem. *A Better Life* is addressed to those among us who were not born in

the UK, but managed to get here in hopes of *A Better Life*. Douglas pours his empathy onto the page and creates a well-written, fantastically structured piece which 100% deserved a podium position.

As I said at the beginning, there's no right or wrong answer to poetry. It's something that I personally love to do, and I know from first-hand experience that it's not everyone's cup of tea. Being a judge for this competition was incredibly humbling for me. It's not something I've ever done before, but I will jump on the opportunity if it is ever presented to me again in the future. Being able to read, indulge and digest dozens of poems by so many creative individuals was an absolute delight. I urge all the poets to continue to spread awareness on racism, inside and outside of the workplace through any medium possible.

Quotable Quotes

When we're talking about diversity, it's not a box to check. It is a reality that should be deeply felt and held and valued by all of us.

Ava DuVernay

Our diversity is our strength. What a dull and pointless life it would be if everyone was the same.

Angelina Jolie

It's really important to share the idea that being different might feel like a problem at the time, but ultimately diversity is a strength.

Carson Kressley

FOREIGN BODY

By Serena Malcolm

Sometimes I forget that I am black.
British girl raised
with a knack
for eloquence
for inoffence
to blend
and bend
and mould inside my brown skin husk,
So 'she' can become one of 'us'
Not quite coconut
but close enough
to appease
and to please,
Culturally bleached just enough
to allow others to relax,
And I too relax,
But then

- SMACK! -

My armour cracks
as my foreign body
is attacked
by a white blood cell
Someone
has
told
a
joke
And I am felled,

And all the rubber necks have snapped,
Breath held back,
Fingers tap
as they wait for me to react...
knuckles crack
In ten seconds flat I:
• realise why
• internally roll my eyes
• sigh
• readjust my guise and
• step up to bat
Here we go again
Here again I must
pretend
or defend,
And though I intend
not to altercate
as I autoplay
(from the pre-selected tracks)
a tune most
attuned
to smooth and tack,
Like verbal Shellac,
I
really
really
really
want to snap,
But in my mind,
Every time,
Right there
at the back,

I hear the whispered
histories
that even made it
p o s s i b l e
for me to snap,
And I rein it back.
Sometimes I forget that I am black.

EQUALITY, DIVERSITY, INCLUSION & ME...

By Poetry Girl

I've worked in global spaces,
With different races and many faces…
The more diverse the workforce community seems to be,
the less diverse is the reality!

1st strike, I'm a woman, 2nd strike, I'm not white, I wonder what
the 3rd strike could be about…
Monday to Friday, I pretend not to be me, only
on Saturday and Sunday can I truly be free…
My face doesn't fit, maybe that's it…It always seems like I have
to be smarter, I need to be stronger, and what's more, I have to
work for longer.

I wonder if there'll ever be true equality, is diversity a pipe dream,
does inclusion include me? A level playing field is all I need.
I should be able to talk to a black colleague, without feeling
the accusing stares boring into my soul.
Feeling like I need to circulate but I gravitate to those to whom
I can relate…

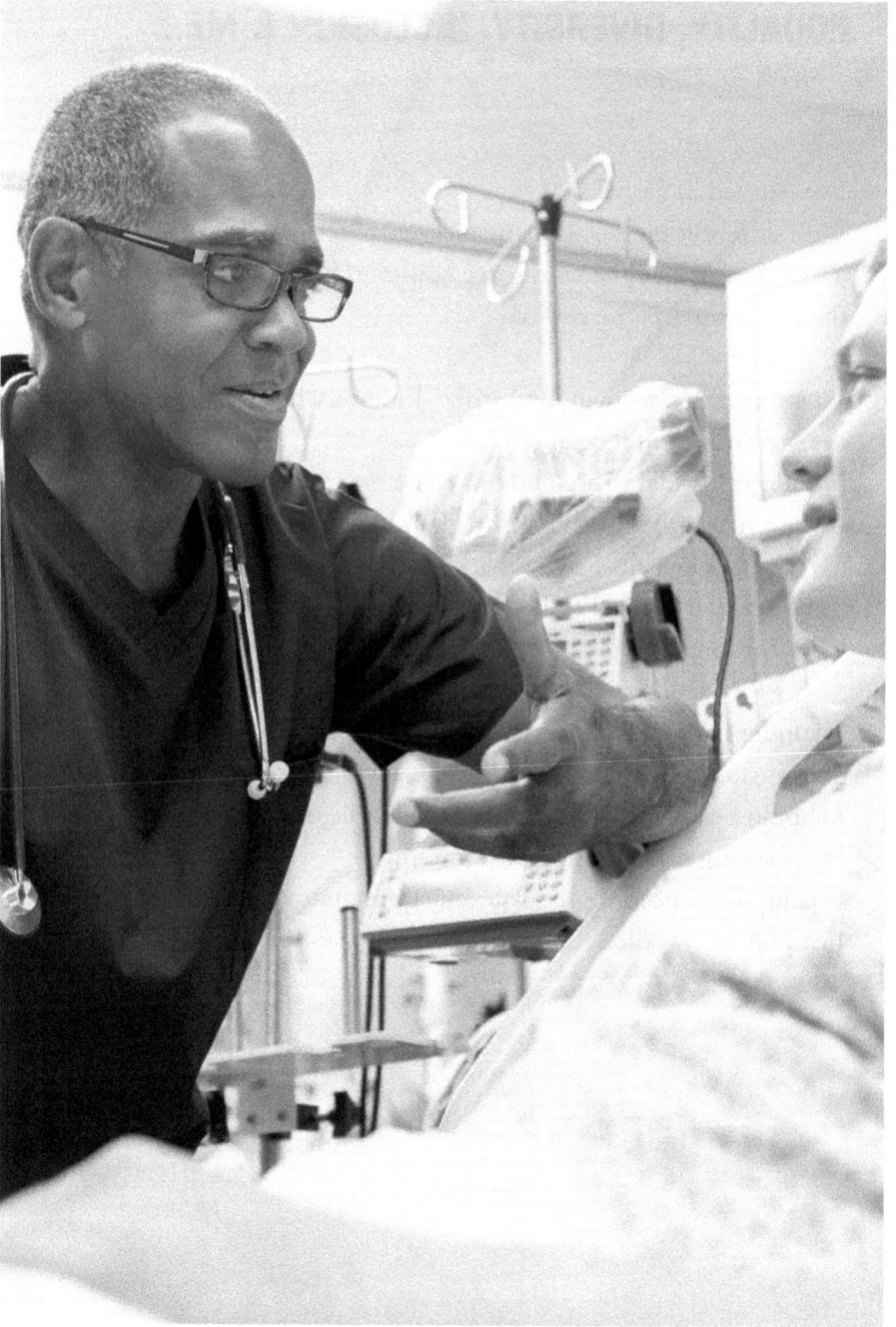

A BETTER LIFE

By Douglas Kingsley Medland

You came here for a better life,
And to feed your family.
Back home you were a doctor,
Here, you're just another refugee.

They held you at the border,
Said we didn't have the space.
Another desperate soul in need,
Turned away because of race.

And when they eventually let you in,
You were shocked at what you saw.
The land of hope and freedom,
Locked in a colour war.

A place where black means poor,
And white means right,
Immigrants feared and put to flight,
Racist agendas on both the left and right.
And you think to yourself,
Am I seeing this right?

Is this the land of liberty?
Where my ancestors fought for the right to be free?
The civil rights movement and I have a dream?
It doesn't look much like it to me.

But despite the way we treat you,
You're still helping to treat us.
We wouldn't let you be a doctor,
So you became a nurse.
And every day I watch you,
Smiling through your shift.
Taking care of those who are,
Most in need of it.

And though we may not show it,
Our country needs you now.
We need to live a better life,
So thanks for showing us how.

SECTION 5:

Poetry Competition:
Highly Commended Poems

The following 25 poems were those that were selected as highly commended entries by the *Black in White Poetry Competition 2021* judges. In selecting these poems, we went for those that made the most impact and were specifically about or could be relevant in a workplace context.

The poems are listed in alphabetical order, based on the poem titles. They cover a wide range of workplace topics and situations, including some by different people of colour – for the record, our poetry competitions are inclusive, and no race or colour is excluded. Notably, a second poem by our first prize winner Serene Malcolm also made it into the highly commended section.

A LIFE NOT THEIR OWN

By Miguel Gabbidon

I could only imagine what it felt like for my forefathers and
mothers to be working in di field day in and day out.
Bending and breaking their backs, cutting, and slashing sugar cane.
While dem mind guh insane, just to labour in vain.
di sun burns dem guh and di rain wet them cum.

But how surreal it must have been, di feeling of their lives being so dim.
They were nothing but a prey, forced to obey.
Betrayed by their own, shackled and bound, dem live a life
not their own,
but no man is an island yet dem stand alone.

Navigated away from dem very home, deprived of dem culture,
Enslaved by vultures. Is this di real human nature?
Tortured when captured, and was taught agriculture, to feed di vultures.
This rapture was a deadly factor that came wid an overseer,
one dem call master.
But if dem try as much as fi relax, it was di cracking sound of di whip,
swish,
swash and that's a lash across their backs.

Leaving the silent tracks of the terror attacks and di hardship dem face,
because dem live ah life not their own. Working their fingers to di bone,
unable to utter a sound, in fear to leave di compound.
Mothers was bound as cattle to the ground, while men lose their head,
children were bred as valuable assets to replenish
the plantation population
but their young heart palpitations were distorted.

By the abuse and trauma, they witness first-hand, suffering from
malnutrition and other illnesses got the best of them.
While mothers and fathers tend to di field children were left to fend for
themselves, rather to spend the master's and doctors recommend it
was the end.
It seemed like a trend that they descend as a savage to the ground.

Though they were born in bondage, they're seldom thinking of
freedom was merely a bliss; they could only escape in their minds.
Yet after a long hard day working in di fields, dem could only unwind
to the taste of a sweet run dung, as the sun goes down.
Their chants and dancing, the cool refreshing taste of a planter's punch,
to quench their thirst, still it couldn't erase or stop an outburst of the
fact that dem live a life not their own.

A SAFE SPACE

By The Poetry Lagoon

My body scrunches up like an old medieval sorcerer
my head bowed down
not in respect but my eyes keep being glued to the ground
fearing the unknown as I walk through the front door
trying not to take any space
I exist in angst
twitching at the sound of every flickering fluorescence
aversion to the faint stale coffee scent
where the congregation gathers
avoiding morning awkward conversations because of "black small talk"
wondering what other races speak about when I am not around
maybe I am just being paranoid
but my tie feels like a noose around my neck
as I struggle to breathe, nor can I utter my identity into existence
out of fear of being rejected
I guess, I will be your negro-lite
your regular James Baldwin of modern times
sacrificing my pride to empathize with your pride
birthed to make white people feel comfortable
help free you from your own guilt for the sake of your egos
just so you can go back to your friends
let them know you are close to a black man
and pat yourself on the back
the responsibilities of your victim
and please, don't ask me why I play along
because I am part of the problem
or maybe I am just exhausted
and maybe ignorance can ease the pain even just for a moment
but only just for a moment.

AN EASY MISTAKE TO MAKE

By Ellie Herda-Grimwood

You introduce your friend to us
with ease, such a breeze,
and you introduce white colleagues
to my right and to my left.
Then you turn to me,
and freeze,
your breath hitching on a wheeze,
as the mode of fight or flight
invites your might in light degrees.

For some godforsaken reason you look fearful,
almost tearful,
as you dart and dive and try to dredge
through your white privilege
for my name,
fairly easy name,
only ever the same.

You stare at me, I stare at you,
you stutter and splutter, and start to utter
but then you angrily mutter
that you've forgotten my name.

...you've *forgotten* my name?

Up, up, begins the burning,
boiling,
churning,
toiling,
rising flame.

A colleague answers to try and tame
this conundrum,
so tiresome,
so dull,
so mundane.

It's been years and years but I'm still fair game,
though it seems as though you feel a *bit* of shame,
so, I guess,
as ever,
"All is forgiven!"
you're none the wiser and I'm left misgiven.

Or so I thought.
If only I'd known what I'd soon be taught.

My stomach's in knots,
my cheeks are hot,
my smile is taut,
I'm feeling fraught,
yet still you insist on having me sought,
and my thoughts are shot
by the rot you've brought.

To my face you draw nearer,
eagerly making it clearer
that you'll happily bind me,
confine me,
so kindly,
and remind me that I'm actually *pretty much* to blame,
but of course, I'm to blame!
Always the same.

You sidle up
and lean in with an aim
to confide and explain
how you came to misname.
Seeing one other girl,
(also brown)
overcame you.
An obvious confusion!
So clear and so plain,
you had absolutely no choice but to blend us,
no worries whatever that you might offend us,
or cause such damage to irrevocably bend us,
ensuring
our inferiority
rears its *ugly* head
to apprehend us.

And in an attempt not to make it worse,
your words have an effect so adverse
that I can do nothing but unhappily traverse
to a miserable memory universe,
full of terse words and lips pursed
when I bemuse *you* by being diverse.
You think you're the first to be averse?
However only ever me,
expected to reverse
and reimburse.

You earnestly claim that it was
such
an
easy
mistake

to make,
and I thought you knew me but
I'm put in my place,
and whilst your words defame me,
your ignorance shames me,
as you talk
and you take
and you talk
and you take,
and as your words start to smother me,
you obliviously
endlessly
continue
to Other me.

And so,
in your increasing attempts not to inflame me,
the only thing you've really done?

Devastatingly
maim me.

BAME

By Jenny Mitchell

He slams me back, the security guard
who prowls outside shoves my naked body
till I stumble on the institution steps.

His hands are wet with ink. Their judgements,
etched across my form from head to toe
by my own hand, turn brown skin black.

The words are small but make their mark,
Your face just doesn't fit twinned on both cheeks,
All service staff are BAME placed on the chin.

One statement round my neck is tight as rope,
Your lot don't socialise in the same way.
It's how we do our deals, you understand?

I've scrawled this last excuse across my breasts.
They, like the other words, are almost prized,
a way to show I never had a chance.

My will to be promoted only proved,
I'm what they always said uncivilised.
This verdict from a boss wends down my back.

She said it more than once straight to my face,
till it's repeated at the meeting of my thighs.
They chaff. When I walk, do they see an ape?

More guards run down the steps, call like baboons.
They push until I sprawl on paving stones, shout
I must be mad to show my body in the cold.

As I attempt to stand, display the hurt,
guards force me to the ground again, stamp
my throat till every word has turned to dust.

BROWN GIRL

By Ansuya Patel

Brown Girl in the ring
the guy from work sang,
grinning like a hero in front
of his work mates.

I was pressured to mingle
after my first week in a new
job. *She looks like a sugar*
in a plum, plum, plum.

Not taking his eyes off my
caramel thighs, drinking
me in as he did his pint
in a few long slurps.

As I stepped out of Bank
tube station, suited men
ogled, stared then followed
me into the office.

Where are you from?
North London I'd say.
No, where are you really
from? I'd scream inside.

Mars, Jupiter, Anus.
I'm Indian. Their eyes
took me in like I was some
exotic creature who'd landed

at my desk. I'd catch their
eyes on me as I walked around
the office, white faces quizzed
my face, questioning my

presence in their space. I left
quickly after making tea,
said hello and looked away,
not stumbling over my interior

rules. Then I saw him, from
the bar who sang those words
that could have destroyed
me, *fancy a drink?*

DEAR KAREN, DEAR KEN

By Neree McKenzie

Dear Karen, Dear Ken,

RE: Exhausted, drained and strained

I hope you can sleep at night knowing full well you've attacked
another black life.
Do you understand the deep-rooted pain and strife we have to
live through each day with negative barriers in our way.

It should be a crime to act the way and say the things that you
do after all it's hell you put us through.

You may not see or believe it is true as day by day we live in fear
of people like you. People like you try to block us from building
in wealth, health, even in the lowest paid areas that generate
growth in the economy.

We play a game, a game that builds pain. Now the gloves are off,
and we well and truly have had enough.

We cannot sit back and allow you to treat us like dirt, causing
more anxiety and hurt. Inferior to who? You?

No Karen, no Ken, let me break it down to you.

Never came to be a favourite, the only thing to be favoured is
the service I provide to help, save up for the biggest purchases
in life, put food on the table for my family and I.

You see, we are mansion beings with shining exteriors and interiors. Expensive in many ways, no you will not a get a refund of how you have always treated us silently or openly.

Yours sincerely

Exhausted, really, and truthfully

HUMMUS AND BREADSTICKS

By Yomn Al-Kaisi

"How do you think the reports went?"
I thought that that your stupid comments in track changes were ignorant and irrelevant.
"They could've gone a little more smoothly."
William, or "willy" as his male colleagues often referred to him, had the patronising look of a man who thought he was being sincere. He was, as his own development goals had set out, 'actively listening'.
Willy takes in a deep breath, sits more deeply into his chair, smiles superficially at the waiter pouring Moroccan mint tea, and continues.
"I think it was, on some level, a frustrating process for all of us."
Bravo Willy! The first layer of your feedback sandwich.
"However..."
Come on Willy, you can do this – you were born to manage people.
"I think that – and feel free to disagree with this — that there were moments where you just wanted it to be over, and as a result quality control suffered."
Last layer of the sandwich William, last layer.
"In any case, the reports have been submitted and that's what matters."
This is probably a dream come true isn't it, Willy? Working in a central London office, working on 'exotic' parts of the word.
"Anyway! Why don't we order some Hummus and breadsticks? They do some great Hummus here."
Not only do you know more about reports on the Middle East than an Arab woman with a graduate degree dedicated to the study of the region, but you think a generic central London Hummus is excellent and ought to be eaten with breadsticks.

"Look, I understand. Working with stakeholders for reports in the Middle East and North Africa can be…. challenging…."

That's right Willy, we're a challenging 465 million.

"In fact, the team and I were impressed with how you dealt with some of those more difficult characters."

Oh yes, those pesky Arabs. They have difficult letters and keep fighting among themselves.

"You know William, I've never tried Hummus and breadsticks. Sounds interesting."

INTERVIEW

By Jacquline Munro

She fumbled
And I stumbled
I choked when she spoke
The words that dribbled
Irresponsibly
Or was
It deliberately
From her lips
Her eyes were questionable
Unashamed when I looked
Was she aware
I swear HR
Would declare
That under the discrimination act
She would have been sacked
In fact, I could have sued
Not come back
Retire
Expire
My working years
She could not understand
The knowledge I possessed
Ten out of ten
A hundred percent
In the test
But the words
That I heard
When she should have been
Offering me the job

Marketing sales extraordinary
Stock exchange millionaires
Revenue I would have increased
What she was worried about
Was
What would the clients say
About my hair
Well I'll be dammed
I declared
Yes, my dread locks are beautiful
But it's me as a person
Who is going to be having the conversation
Negotiating
No deliberating
To seal the deal
Wrap up the contract
Which would have an unprecedented impact
Instead she was concerned
What the clients
Would say about my hair
I looked at the blonde nest
That sat in front of me
Behind the desk
Perplexed
At this black beauty
Whose qualification
Was not the issue
Whose ability to
Accumulate clients
In the highest position
Job upheld
She thought she was in her right

No apology
No discrimination review
Diversity and inclusive
Acts facts
None of that
I waited
Giving her room
To retract her question
To react the scene
Act two which she did not rehearse
Did not think she needed to converse
I smiled
I looked at the time
It was only
Quarter past nine
She clocked
That I was looking at my watch
Was she really waiting for the answer
To the question that she
That she used as her prop
My natural dread locks
Was the issue
It had become the main suspect
Of this crime
Was she trying
To evaluate my immediate state
Digress in her foolishness
Her ignorance
Or was this a prank
I was not going to entertain this
Articulately I responded
I had no time to joke

Obviously, I am too good for this role
A black woman's hair
Has exceeded all expectations
Beyond your wit
Beyond your categories
Your boxes of questions that you tick
Thank you
For a very interesting interview
One of the best in fact
As I am intrigued
That someone of your calibre
Is still employed here
I wonder what your HR
Or more interestingly
Your CEO
Would think of that
Goodbye
I look forward
To the letter in the post
With my results of the interview
And don't forget to include your feedback
That's what I will enjoy most

LANES AND RACES

By Cece Noel

You say that you expect more from me,
Implicitly saying
That black women like me are expected to work
10 times harder.
Normal status quo standards do not suffice
When it's my efforts as the subject line -
The progress bar slows to a crawl.
You expect me to pedal faster
To gain the same distance as my peers on the same track,
Because it's the same track but a different race -
Same ground covered but different lanes;
Lanes with potholes,
Continuous uphill terrain,
Unrelenting, steadfast obstacles,
And character assassinations.
My eyes are now open.

My skin is now raw to the touch.
My joints and limbs ache
With age beyond my years,
Yet I won't stop running. I refuse to stop running.
My open eyes can look around
But I also keep looking forward,
To prove that your head would be spinning
If you were to run in my lane.
So I keep looking forward,
Because that is what I expect from myself.

LETTER TO SISLIN

By Capability; Black

I'm sorry to hear I missed you, there's a few things I need to say,
I'm writing you from London, so many, many miles away.

I've stepped into the footprints you trod, all those years ago,
how grateful we are aunty; you will never truly know!

It must've been so difficult, being first, the only one,
being British but still "a farin" and into service you did come.

I want to tell you aunty, that my uniform was always smart,
my trousers pressed, my boots high shine, and very eager to start.

I felt so proud and walked so tall, well I am tall enough,
and with each step, had to 'member that you too did have it tough.

I ignore the looks, the sneers, the whispers and many a rude remark,
racial tropes, straight up foulness, hiding hurt inside my heart.

I walked the beat, and rode in cars, blue lights and sirens wailing,
every moment, trusting that my people, I wasn't failing.

our men can't walk in the street aunty, without a Stop or "where you
going, please?"
it's every day,
it's all the time,
like London "nah fi we"

we always fayva someone or fit description of some nex' man,
there or not, that aint the point, **they're** suspicious and **we** look like
we can.

they say it's the whole institution now and not just a bad few,
that call us names and treat us bad and over scrutinise what we do.

"we aren't as good; we aren't as smart and when we talk, we mek a fuss."
despite the image that is shown, trust, it's always "them" and "us"

I'm really trying aunty, to protect the weak and help the good,
to uphold the oath, your image, your memory, as I want to - As I should.

I wanted to send better word, 'bout how we're making out,
it's hard to hide and play pretend when the news shows what we're about.

We killed a Brother; his name was George, in the States the other day,
a brave girl filmed it, the video went viral, as we watched him slip away.

It was a lynching, just horrible and delivered under foot,
my heart ached and my eyes filled up, watching us create "Strange Fruit"

the uniform felt heavier, with embarrassment and pain,
every day,
every hour since,
asking "Why'd I do this?" again

I'm glad you can't see us, because if you did, you definitely would,
see that we're still only passing through, that much is understood.

we pretty up their imagery, so they don't look homogenised,
the colour is good, so do come in, but "leave your Blackness outside!"

we dared to hope, I met her once… the tunnel, is she "that" light?
but on and on, the wheels keeping turning; wrong, despite what's right.

we look for you (in vain, always) and speak up your name often,
we anchor to your story, so brave, to ensure you aren't forgotten.

they've gathered up and grouped us, in this stupidness called "BAME"
to disappear the demonic Black, "don't call them by that name".

bureaucratic paper cuts have consequence, and are lethal,
the systems, the policies discriminate, and more so for us Black people.

we go backwards, and forwards, to go backwards again,
forgetting the passage made for us, by you; our Aunt Sislin.

I started out naively, wanting "an honest job for an honest pay"…
but this here aint for Black people, only keeping things the white way.

we feel conflicted, and it's getting worse, our prognosis; it's too far gone,
all o' we, be witnessing, "the fall of Babylon".

I'll sign off cos you're resting, your shift over and years gone by,
we're stony faced by what we've seen and in private we might cry.

but tell me something aunty, help us, with a sign, a message or clue.
How do we maintain, stand fast like you did, when we are Black
and in this Blue?

MY NAME, MY SURNAME, MY BIRTHNAME

By Broken Glass

My name is my curse,
My name is my block,
My name – my name,
My name can be punishment.

If only I had a chip on my shoulder,
If only I got an interview,
If only my qualification were equal,
If only my vibrating air sounds like yours.

You're in the wrong room
this is the interview for a new lecturer.
Let me justify myself.
You're so articulate.

I applied for ninety-nine vacancies, and none got back to me,
I tried for so long, but like a lost soul on the ocean – I lost hope,
I decided to sink my boat as I couldn't see land – how to cope,
I reside to swim - chocking on the sea of discrimination, it did me.

The subtle brutality of the unread application unqualified by my
surname,
My name is against me, my surname my mental shackling,
Your name is so hard to pronounce, is that G?
My name, my surname, my birthname – a tool made to drive me insane.

MY TRUE NAME

By Yurika Nemoto-Smith

Short
Sweet
Unknown
Those blunt letters defined me

Years of my life being called another name
Because you couldn't pronounce it

I changed because of you
I was unknown because of you

Cut down to become someone else
Abbreviated for the ease of everyone else

What about me? Did you ask if it was easier for me?

When you wanted to know I told you. And you laughed –
Said it was
        Weird

            Too long

                How the fuck am I meant to pronounce that?
Don't you have an easier one?
*Don't you have an **English one?***

So I adapted, I shortened, I changed

Because of you

You butchered my name. You slaughtered who I was –
To hear you say it so
                    Gutturally
                                        So dismissively

            You offended my ears

You didn't even try
But I met people who did

That's why I kept it. My ears now hear the beauty in my
Short
Sweet
Unknown name

I'm glad you will never know my true name

NEW JOB

By Jennifer Shaw

Once during my teaching career
It was my first day I fear
Although I had multiple jobs
I was to be at this job at daylight
But when I arrived… I got a serious fright

The alarm in the building began to sound
Because someone had been trying to penetrate the grounds
Breaking through the silence
Although I was standing there alone
Someone called the police on the phone

After the police was called
The policeman arrived on the scene quick
He immediately pulled out his nightstick
I didn't expect what happened next
So… I was standing there sending a text

Even after I told him who I was
The police let it be known he had some suspicion
That's when he made me assume the position
He decided I had to be up to no good
Then he made me put my hands on his hood

Although I told him I was there to work
He proceeded to act like some kind of jerk
He took some handcuffs off his belt
He placed them tightly on my hands behind my back
Then calling the station he said, "I got the criminal… She's Black"

I was surprised at his racist remarks
Just standing there with an angry look on my face
I wasn't sure if I wanted to work at that place
Just at that moment my boss pulled up
She demanded that he remove his cuffs

He began to explain to her
That I had shown him an I.D. that wasn't real
Because I had to be at school that early just to steal
You can't imagine my surprise
When she mouthed "I'm sorry" while looking into my eyes

My boss assured him he was wrong
That I was right where I belonged
I often wonder to this day
If our skin had been the same colour
Would things have turned out the same way

I was really appalled
The police didn't apologize at all
He was quick to say
No harm… no foul
However, for policeman I guess apologies are not allowed

NO COWARD SOUL AM I

By Emma Conally-Barklem

A knock at the classroom door, morning fugue of teenagers, teacher filled with caffeine -optimism and love of the Brontës.
No, this isn't African Studies, starched pause, lambent air of embarrassment as woke students snigger, Jeez Miss, really?

I mean really?

Did I hear clearly?

Incredulous swallowed back shock, swearing solidarity from cynical white youth, the truth of this racism archaic as chalk on a board.
He really did say that, but there's no such thing on the syllabus, so was he just taking the piss or trying to dismiss my right to educate in the ways of literature,
Histrionic female mulatto has no rights here, in the hallowed halls of Shakespeare, did you think education would clear, the decks for respect?
I continue, defiant as Emily knowing the remedy is me imperious, brim full of books and passion, no rash reaction, instead going higher, words as swords,
So fall back anachronistic tutor as I sally forth into a new future.

PEDESTRIAN CROSSINGS

By Eleni Cay

Her hair doesn't fly, but swings,
as if she had an extra limb
to fight for being a black woman.
She sits next to a white man.

His dark suit seems to be asleep,
but the luminous screen on his wrist
is fully alive: there are five red
dots indicating time.

She wears bold colours, they're easier
to clean. Her five bright toenails in half-
torn flipflops laugh loud among all the
sheltered feet on a packed morning train.

They both get off at St Pancras,
turn into opposite directions,
then cross again at the gate.
They don't register that they are
sustained by the same shade of red.

'RACE IS NO LONGER AN ISSUE?'

By Osaremen Iluobe

'Race is no longer an issue'
Well, that's what we hear
But through experience, learning, and growing each year
I came to the realization that,
This wasn't true
In a supposedly meritocratic nation,
The land of red, white, and blue
The flag that once stood as a symbol for liberty and violence
A symbol so contradictory, that even today some may try silence
For drawing attention to the truth, the legacy of past days
And now they question why it's a struggle to accept
My Britishness in whole ways
In ways that extend beyond a care for Euro 2020
The booing of the players encouraged by politicians aplenty
Race is no longer an issue
Is perhaps easy to say if you're ignorant of facts
But the truth of the matter is
The opposite is true if you're black.

SECOND GUESSING

By Aretha Ahunanya

Call me an over-thinker.
Many things pass through my mind that you might not consider
A culmination of experiences, traumas, triggers —
Forcing me to question what is 'privilege'?
As I navigate a world that decided I'm different.

Some can enter any room and not feel out of place
Not searching for a face which looks kind of like theirs,
Ignoring the piercing stares
Which make you feel as though you're not meant to be there

I wonder what it's like
To never fear being a stereotype
To never silence the words in your mind
Code-switching language
From family to friends
Giving no one a 'reason' to doubt your intelligence.

I wonder, do they know?
What it's like to be surrounded and alone?
Assimilating to a dialect you barely know
Leaving culture back home
Because God forbid, someone label you 'ghetto'

Choosing which aspects of myself to neglect
If I could just correct —
How I speak, how I dress,
I might escape the single image
Of the black girl they expect.

But instead

I choose myself.
To the highest level of authenticity,
Ignoring desperation for conformity
Because I deserve to simply **be**.

Perhaps, this has never crossed your mind
For some will never feel the need to re-define themselves
Day after day
But for others like me,
The conflict remains

SOJOURNER

By Isabel Aruna

Chapter 1: Dad

Feel my story.
It's not about whether I can do the job, it's about who I am.
The skin I sit in, its beautiful consequences chase me.
No, I'm not being paranoid. Of course, you see colour, so do I.
I'm judged before I even walk into a room.
But my face still shines with strength and pride that can never
be dimmed.

You struggle to pronounce the name of the
hallowed halls which grew my great mind.
Fed my hunger.
But the award wasn't enough. Not here.
Leaving the scars of Sierra Leone's civil war, I came seeking
a better future,
but was treated like the cleaner you expected me to be.
It's hard to remember how I was once esteemed.

But it wasn't just you.
I felt the stake from others in different shades, other races,
people who knew what it felt like to be a foreigner on this ground.
But their words never killed me.
I wondered, can there ever be unity with us? Can we really stand as one?
Shouldn't we be friends?
You all didn't hear my roar for more.

So, I learnt how to play your game better than you
and learnt a niche so in demand I could no longer be ignored.
I taught my daughters to do the same.
I whispered sweet wisdom in their ears to help secure them.
Now look at how tall I have become.

I studied your language then watched your tongue.
My accent that you once used to crush me has no chains anymore,
now its glory is revealed to family back home.
But now even with my pristine, who do you favour?
Younger pearlier treats than me.
I've risen, but how do I move this glass ceiling that you've put above me?
It's so hard to smash.
Oh, I'm not looking to belong, I know where my real home is.
One day soon, I'll take what I have built with these bare hands
and return.

Chapter 2: Mum

Feel my story.
I came here from a village in Kenya with just five pounds to spare.
Hustled for more but was given a red mark against my name,
as soon as you saw my baby recoil at your touch.
That mark crushed my hopes of creating room
for the imagination of innocent joys.

I fell into caring for the frail and rolled into its unfair insecurity.
26 years and what do I have to show for it?
Why do you treat them differently to me? Treat them...better.

When my buns in the oven grew, my pack retreated from London life
to a bigger spread outside of the ring.
Now we could hire builders and cleaners
for the windows of our new two-story house.
Yes, we finally owned it, it was ours.
But some of you turned us away,
you were disgusted to work for our expresso magnificent spirits.
You'd rather not get paid for your job than be employed by me?

I found new work and was welcomed with open arms
to different shades of the same.
Some clients don't even want me to touch them.
They'd rather get no help than mine.
My employer buries internal racist complaints under the carpet,
most of the time.

The image of us that dominates in your mind is much
angrier, louder, and aggressive than the truth.
Why are you so surprised that I'm so calm and composed?
Who do you think I am?
You'll use me if I let you, and you won't recognise the best of my skills
too.
Maybe it a ploy to keep me under your thumb,
to stop me from roaring louder.

Chapter 3: Me

Feel my story.
My friends, let me tell you a piece of the truth that you can't ever see,
even with a mirror.
I grew up learning, ''you have to work twice as hard to get half of what
they have ''
Did you?
Believe me it's true, I mean did you know
that I'm at least twice more likely to be unemployed than you?

I remember the otherness I felt when people
are surprised that I speak English so well.
Sometimes much finer than you.
Am I used as a token or a model to show that the impossible is possible?
But it's hard. Harder than it should be.

I remember when I was summoned into a meeting that felt like a trap.
Did you even listen to me?
Or did you just hear her behind her seniority and power?
A work-life balance is healthy. It's what humans need.
But that luxury hasn't been bestowed onto us
when we need to stay two steps ahead of the game.
My mother laughs at the idea.
Sometimes you should see why some of us have found
the best self-preservation is silence.
It's not tolerance, it's just so draining having to justify our truth,
battling with the face of your white fragility and deaf ears.

So rarely is my ebony skin risen up for its excellence,
and it is so excellent. But sometimes I'm just seen as good for my own.
I don't want to be one of the best young upcoming black females in my
field.
I just want to be one of the best youngsters in my sector full stop.
These categories. I'm nearly always in a widening participation category.

How my people birth riches that should be celebrated,
instead, we are given a month.
October has never tasted so bitter like the year of 2021
with the memory of George burned in our brains.
But there has always been more, so much more innocent blood shed
by the authority and more, that demand us to submit
but are meant to serve and protect us.
Although our ancestors paved the way for us to reach for higher,
we can still pay with our lives in these modern days.

Oh, don't get me wrong, I do appreciate your concern believe me,
black lives do matter.
But why are you only looking now?
Why is the richness of your white privilege finally hitting home now?
Will you shake the foundations of the institutional racism that is
entrenched within?
The one that paves the way
for microaggressions and unconscious biases to name a few.
Will things start to change now for the better?
Or will you just close your eyes and fall back asleep?

SOLICITED

By Gabrielle Felix

Equally qualified
equally comprehended
essays prized
letters well read
a façade of same stead
until their eyes affix to my hair
my skin, my dress
dread
when I open my mouth
words no longer poignant
and an accent lingers instead
as they question
whether I am the representor or
represented.

THE 3 BLACK LIONS

By Patrick Edore

3 lions fell
3 lions will rise once again
I will remain loyal regardless

We Blacks are British
...when we score
Foreigners, when we miss

It's time to rise
Time to unite
England, oh England
Show us how Great Though Art

THE BLACK CEILING

By Jhiselle Feanny

Here I am, looking up, the sky's the limit, but please don't touch!

It's not for you, it's just for them, not for your kind, you are condemned.

I stare above the glass so high, I look, can't touch as they transcend.

Why don't they look at all like me? I should progress, fly high, be free?

I fly above the blackened sky, the ceiling points for them, not I?

My race, my gender, my class denied… success and progression that they decide.

I hit the ground I stumble on, lost hope, regret of who I am. I drift and wonder my reason to live. To touch the sky, believe and give.

Oh no, not me, I will achieve, and breakthrough chains designed to weave, a history to oppress and control, but not upon my mortal soul.

And here she is, above the cloud, the sky so near above the crowd. Above the norm, I won't conform, I have achieved, I have transformed.

The ceilings gone, and so are they, I now achieve my equal pay.

I stand, I watch, as others touch, that sky above, I crave so much.

Equality is all I see, my place to stay, to rest and be. This is the norm, we all are free, they give me an apology.

It's free, it's safe, not judged by race, and those right here all earned their place.

It's guaranteed adversity, above the black ceiling, diversity!

TICK BOX

By Leeanne Parke

If you want some boxes ticked, I'm ideal,
A living walking definition of swirl.
It's tough to express how it feels;
The silent judgement and senseless attack.
Too black to be white,
Too white to be black.
A stranger in the land of my birth,
Shock when I'm well spoken with self-worth.
Never knowing if I'm just fulfilling a quota,
Having to pretend I don't care an iota
Because I want to fit in. The irony,
When I was picked precisely because I don't.
The world moves faster than attitudes can adjust.
I have faith there will be change,
In humanity I trust

TOKEN BLACK FRIEND

By Serena Malcolm

Always
on
my best behaviour,
Just smile and keep their favour
no matter what the labour
- Don't offend -
Even if you must pretend,
You have to act like them,
Laid way, way back,
So I don't snap,
Compact
that stereotype
of just another angry black,
Hair kept on track
in tracks,
Or on the straight and narrow
- relaxed -
Ever chasing that tell-tale shake
that tell-tells my sisters
I got the good stuff,
Not the hood stuff
that burns and breaks,
Or I've got that afro sheen
that's somewhere in between
dry and greasy
so when They ask
Can I touch it?
Is it sheepy?
They don't have to be uneasy,
Sleazily wiping their palms

in secret disgust,
Not that I should be fussed;
I didn't ask to be touched,
Violated
by their microaggressive
hatred
Each time they ask:
Are you two related?
Or ask who I've dated
and then:
Oh I don't mean to be crude,
but are rumours true?
How would I have a clue?
I don't know
every
black
man,
Do you?
Oh, for the more subtle
enquires about
the food that I eat...
I always feel the need
to say
Well, I love shepherd's pie!
I don't know why,
I guess it's easier
than that uneasy eye
when I'm forced to describe
cassava leaves,
or rice and peas,
or okra with tripe,
You eat tripe?!

Yep, that's right.
And what music I like?
Well, all sorts!
I say,
Downplay the blackness
of my tastes,
Make myself eclectically swayed,
Culturally greyed,
Just to allay their discomfort,
White-wash
my essence,
Scrub out the presence
of my ethnicity,
Well, apart from the melanin you can see,
For fear of being devalued
- or worse -
Degraded,
Paraded around like a curiosity,
A collector's item
with the highest finder's fee,
A quaint little rarity,
Come and see my
afro-bearing,
chicken-loving,
hip-hop-hearing
neck-snapping,
head scarf-wearing
token black friend,
Isn't she a gem?

WE GOT THIS

By Kate Meyer-Currey

We've rolled together
All my life, Mr Shame.
Guess I'd say
It's complicated.
Even friends
With benefits.
Just when I think
I'm free at last
You rock up
On side, when
Mean girl society
Takes a pop:
I'm that bitch
Who needs
A lesson.
You know me
Better than
They do.
You were my
Silent witness
Many times
Before
When the crowd
Turned on me.
As I was kicked
Catcalled
Or held accountable
For real
Or fabricated
Transgression.

Only you
Had my back
You taught me
Self-defence.
Thing is, Mr Shame
We own it when
There's no excuse
We know we're guilty;
We hold our hands up
Our faces blaze
Our guts churn
We get foetal
On the couch
Can't leave
The house
We do our
Punishment homework
Our souls
Take stripes.
We comply
To survive.
But seems like
That's not enough
When haters
Hold the reins
Of social conformity:
In life and work.
We stand out
We're easy targets
They smell
Our difference

It makes them uneasy
So they throw stones
Or try and drown us
In the river of judgement.
We're better than that
We see us in the round
All that dirty work
Showed us real:
We deflect missiles
We float downstream;
We can still walk tall
We can see through
The smoke and mirrors
Of jurisdiction
Of petty control:
We speak our truth
The naked emperor's
Minions quake
With rage and terror.
The sun shines
For us, too;
We are bold and free:
Let them hide
In the shadows;
Shame on them.

WHERE ARE YOU FROM FROM?

By Rebecca Caine

My father was black, my mother was white
But where are you really from?
My features are black, my skin white at first sight

I can't tell, you Brazilian, from Hawaii?
Neither, I'm no puzzle for your twist
You can tick two boxes you know
But I'm not even on this list!

So how do you feel? Black or white?
That's for me to know, me to find out
I feel sorry for you, you're not one or the other
That's for me to discover, for me to doubt

Where are you from, from?
That's for me to name
Come on, where are you really from?
That's for me to claim

SECTION 6:

About Black in White

Charlotte Shyllon: I started this company to support the publishing and marketing activities for my book of poems, *Black in White*, which describes some of my experiences of racism in the corporate world. I also provide a range of equality, diversity and inclusion consultancy services to companies and organisations, and consult specifically on race issues.

I am fortunate to have a talented team of individuals who support this mission. Read more about each wonderful person on the **Black in White team.**

David P Balfour: David is sometimes called Bally, Baby or even Dave. His corporate role is in IT/Telecoms, currently working on Apps within the Software development arena as a Technical Programme Manager. What he likes most about his role within the Black in White programme planning team is that he gets to work across all elements of the *Black in White* workstreams from brainstorming, planning through to event management, he loves the people interaction. His aims are to give to the community what he has learnt from his personal and corporate experiences in life.

David's favourite quote is *"Man know thyself; then thou shalt know the Universe and God."* – attributed to Pythagoras. His two favourite non-fictional books are: *Make The Most of Your Mind* by Tony Buzan and *A Book of World Religions* by Geoffrey Parrinder. His two favourite fictional books are: *Wave Without a Shore* by CJ Cherryh and *Anansi and Company: Retold Jamaican Tales* by Bish Denham. The values he holds most dear are:

1) What goes around comes around
2) Seeing the good in others or the diamond in the rough

David's guilty pleasure is locking himself away and tinkering with electronics, modifying, improving, or re-imagining a bit of kit.

Debbie a.k.a. Debs or 'Debbie Gadget': Debbie lives in Northwest London with her family. When she's not solving people problems in her day job, she loves to spend time with her family, and enjoys puzzles and games.

Why she's on the Black in White team: The possibility and opportunities to make a difference and the chance to work with a like-minded team. There are no limits.

Favourite quote:

"I've learnt that people will forget what you said, people will forget what you did, but people will never forget how you made them feel."

– Maya Angelou.

Values that drive her: Honesty, equity/fairness, resilience/perseverance.

Top books/written works:

Eats Shoots and Leaves by Lynne Truss – It appeals to the pedant in me!

The New Geography of Jobs by Enrico Moretti – a smart discussion of how different cities and regions have made a changing economy work for them – and how policymakers can lift the circumstances of workers everywhere.

Black in White by Charlotte Shyllon (but of course).

We're going on a Bear Hunt by Michael Rosen & Helen Oxenbury – both of my children loved it and a lot of time was spent reading this and making the required noises and movements.

My 15-year-old daughter's written work: **COoooOoome... COoooOoome...**

Hymns, a sweet voice sang. Like a bird, awakening you from slumber.

The ears, sweetened, yet, the mind, deafened.

Guilty pleasure: Ice cream – the nuttier, the better. Favourite flavours include macadamia, pistachio, almond, cashew, peanut, and coco(nut). Yum!

Denyse Barwick: Trinidadian-born Denyse is an administrator with over 14 years' experience. She has worked with large companies in London and Essex, meeting many people from around the world in both the fashion and motoring industries. A mother of three now young adults, she has been involved in School PTAs, served as a governor, and helped to arrange and stage many school, church, and social events. She volunteered as a manager and chairperson with Harlow Steelband for several years, and still supports them as one of her sons is a member of the band. Steelpan music is one of her many passions as are art and design, event planning, research, interior design and learning about foods from different cultures, including Caribbean, Indian and African dishes.

Charlotte and Denyse attend the same church, and she helped to organise a few events for Charlotte before joining *Transforming Words* for a while as an Executive Assistant. Having worked together on the virtual launch event for *Black in White*, it was a definite "Yes" when she was asked to be a part of this wonderful team again for the poetry competition. Reading is another one of Denyse's many hobbies, so helping to be involved in the publishing and launch of another book is simply fantastic.

Hanna: She's Hanna! Sometimes cheeky, sometimes opinionated but tactful and always friendly and loyal. She currently works part-time as a Project Coordinator in Charlotte's company, *Transforming Words* which gets her into some *Black in White* work too. With a working background in administration, her main passion, however, is anything artistic and handy. She enjoys drawing and painting, papier mache, jigsaw puzzles, Sudoku, and DIY.

Hanna is relishing the opportunity to be involved in *Black in White* and she is beginning to renew her appreciation of the art of poetry, listening more to the words in songs and poems. She has re-read a long-time favourite poem *Shall I compare thee to a summer's day...* sonnet 18 by William

Shakespeare and little snippets that have fired her imagination recently are:

My head's underwater but I'm breathing fine, …
… Love your curves and all your edges,
All your perfect imperfections …. From *All of Me* by John Legend

Have a fabulous day, whatever you're doing!
If it's work, deliver fabulously! …
… Because that's what we are… FABULOUS! From *Fabulous* by Charlotte Shyllon

Hanna is also turning her hand to poetry following a recent experience of knife crime in a park. Everyone is said to have a book in them, maybe everyone has also got a poem in them. Working title is *Another Number* – watch this space!

Sarah Murray: Sarah is from East London. She works within the social care industry as an Advanced Practitioner of Social work and serves within the children ministry of her church Kingsway International Christian Centre, the place where she first met Charlotte Shyllon. Sarah was a young mum at age 18, she believes that her faith in God has helped her in defying the odds and negative pronouncements made against young mums. Sarah loves to encourage and inspire others, while leading by example. Sarah is a mother of four and married to her 'high school sweetheart'.

Sarah is a firm believer in education, gaining and imparting knowledge. This was her foundational principle for joining the *Black in White* planning team in 2020, helping to network, promote *Black in White* and organise various events. Her experiences of racism as a black female underpins her drive to bring about awareness and education around racism whether hidden or blatant, alongside the need for justice and fairness.

Sarah knew from a very young age that she had the ability to help others; she desires to leave people in a better position than she found them in. She is passionate about helping others to build their vision and possess the ability to carry projects to accomplishment.

Tia Miles *(she/her)*: Tia is a 24-year-old from East London. She works in the finance industry as a Reporting Analyst and runs her own digital art business. **Tia Diana Draws©** specialises in custom illustrations, graphic design, animations, cover art and logos.

Tia has been part of the Black in White planning team since 2020, helping to organise various events and even judged *Black in White's* first ever poetry competition! Her poetry journey began at a young age, and she has always enjoyed sharing her work with those around her.

Nowadays, Tia performs poetry and spoken word at open mic events to share her work and spread awareness on – what can be – taboo subjects. *'My Name is Tia'*, which features in this book, is Tia's greatest poetry achievement. This poem was written in May 2020 following the tragic death of George Floyd, to spread awareness about racism and the discrimination Tia has experienced herself as a mixed-race Londoner.

Get in touch

Contact Charlotte if you have any questions about *Black in White*, wish to access any of our products and services, issue an invitation to speak or to discuss collaboration opportunities.

E: **charlotte@blackinwhiteservices.co.uk**

W: **www.blackinwhiteservices.co.uk**

Follow us on Instagram and Twitter: @Blackinwhite27

Subscribe and like our YouTube channel (Charlotte Shyllon)

Winston Lemuel Tennyson Forde
Edited by the WLTF Literary Agency
http://www.winstonfordebooks.com

www.ingramcontent.com/pod-product-compliance
Lightning Source LLC
Chambersburg PA
CBHW072155090426
42740CB00012B/2273